Table of Contents:

<u>**Preface:**</u>

Dear reader,

This book should contribute to a better life through orientation and optimization - a better "code" leads to an emotional gain in society ...

The meaning of life is (basically) to live, whereby feelings (the soul of the person, which you can hear in their voice) are most important. Feelings represent something at the moment in an infinite universe of space and time. Proper nutrition („fuel") is crucial for feelings (salad and pasta are re-commended and 1 x meat or fish per week), as well as always doing the right thing in the moment.

The right action in the current moment is the philosophical way to get to the goal - the equilibrium - which is a state of complete balance and satisfaction - quasi a central zero point in which everything is taken into account and also done - which leads to that one then currently free head can use for the next thing that comes. Establishing a balance (equilibrium) is a wise path that leads to the benefit of equilibrium ...

The focus is on "man and woman" - both act together (balanced, harmonious and complementary), are healthy and have offspring - you can't do it alone, nature has done that (through specialization). For this everyone has to find the right partner, come to an agreement and go together on the way to the goal (the equilibrium), whereby "the way is the goal" (Confucius) - the framework is determined by the majority. Give and take should be the same so that everyone is satisfied ...

Basically all people are the same (at least the dog), but in particular they are not. Rules should give all people the same (action) framework, but who wants to judge that when there are huge differences between people. The fact that people look and are different leads to many different groups that can hardly be brought together, as they are sometimes controversial, but as a whole are very rich due to their colorful diversity, which is advantageous for a common goal of people: That Survival of the species. Democracy means that the current majority determines, but not necessarily, that this is better for everyone (especially for special people). An improvement of this democracy is presented here in the book as "optimized democracy", so that the quality of the choice continues to improve. This might make the rules even more intelligent, diverse and special. But I would like to point out that this idea contains certain risks (classification, outing, etc.) and should only be tested in a longer pilot project (with data protection) ... perhaps one could start with a neutral institute giving a score to politicians.

It should also be taken into account that not all people have the same opportunities in life and that they are "forced" to go the "wrong path" from the start - for example, they lack education, family and work. Here, richer people could give poor children the chance of education, health and a job at the beginning with the help of a development program ...

In addition, it should be said that "it doesn't work out in the end" if the destruction of human, vegetable, animal and other (environmental) resources on the planet costs more "capital" than it currently brings in profit for some industrialists , because their own properties are ultimately worthless if everything (globally) is "broken" ...

A further development of life can mean that the resulting better work makes interstellar space flights and the colonization of other planets possible at some point in the future.

It is certainly wise to ensure that the descendants survive in the long term ...

Mark

<u>**Think:**</u>

The way people think is very different and goes from the individual to the general thinking collective, from simple to complicated / complex matter ...

"Thinking includes all processes that result from an inner preoccupation with imaginations, memories and understood / understanding try to shape. "(Wikipedia). If one compares thinking with a computer process, one could imagine that a program with its instructions is used to logically process the relevant data (from main and permanent memory) in a processor in order to determine a result – but one would have to with people also involve feelings (in a relevant strength).

With the approach of mathematics, thinking becomes correct, and with the help of technology, action becomes logical. However, one should consider everything, ie know everything. What is important for your own life at the moment, "is told by your feelings".

Intuition (intuitio = immediate perception) is the ability to gain insight into facts, points of view, laws or the subjective coherence of decisions without discursive use of the mind, without any conscious conclusions. Intuition is partmore creative developments. The one accompanying the development intellect(the ability to grasp something spiritually, and the authority in humans that is responsible for knowing and think is responsible) only carries out or consciously checks the results that come from the unconscious. It is critical to see here that if a – initially not justifiable – decision has a positive effect, one likes to speak of intuition, while in the case of failure one has simply "made a mistake", whereby there is no mechanism to check which mental processes lead to respective decision. Alcohol, drugs and meat all have an effect. "Some scientists suspect that the information exchange between the"enteric "nervous systemand the brain also has a role to play in making intuitive decisions ("good decisions"). "(Wikipedia). For many, the action is then a habit, depending on what they eat or have eaten ...

<u>**Philosophy:**</u>

1. The meaning of life is to live
2. Life is made up of feelings
3. The feelings arise through action
4. The plot should fit
5. Life is a life's work of actions and feelings
6. "The way is the goal" (Confucius)

<u>Ethics:</u>

"Is that part of the philosophywhich deals with the prerequisites and the evaluation of human action. That is specifically at the center of ethics moral action, especially with regard to its justifiability and reflection". (Wikipedia)

<u>Simple 4-field table for "trading":</u>

TO DO SOME THING UNRIGHT THAT BELONGS (is proper)	TO DO SOME THING RIGHT THAT BELONGS (is proper)
TO DO SOME THING UNRIGHT THAT DOESN`T BELONGS (improper)	TO DO SOME THING RIGHT THAT DOESN`T BELONGS (improper)

TABLE OF GOODNESS		
BE FAIR	BE ALIVE	ACT WISELY
THINK LOGICAL	PROTECT LIFE	MARRY SOMEONE
KNOW EVERYTHING	BE HEALTHY	HAVE CHILDREN
INFORM PEOPLE	THINK COMPLETE	BE HONEST
BE OPEN	MAKE YOUR OWN DECISIONS	BE PUNCTUALLY
BE CREATIVE	ACT RESPONSIBLE	BE ORDERLY
BE TOLERANT	FIND THE MIDDLE	BE CORRECT
MAKE A SHOW	KEEP BALANCE	BE RIGHTEOUSNESS
BE VARIED	BE READY	MAKE SOME MONEY
LIVE FREE	BE ABLE	BE CLEAN
BE CRITICAL	BE CAREFUL	MAKE A DEMONSTRATION
PRESERVE HUMANITY	BE HOLISTIC	BE PRECISE
HELP OTHERS	BUILT A TEAM	INFORM AND TRAIN YOURSELF
	SET UP AN INSTITUTION	LEARN + IMPROVE
	WORK TOGETHER	TEACH OTHERS
	FIGHT FOR EQUITY (FAIRNESS)	

In the end there is the Philosopher's Stone and you become a constellation (role model)

Does "good" actually mean "god"?

(Isn't there a connection?)

<u>**Believe:**</u>

Faith means that one facts is believed to be apparently true, without any methodological justification. Belief in everyday language use is therefore a presumption or hypothesis that assumes the truth of the presumed facts, but at the same time leaves open the possibility of refutation if the presumption changes through facts or new ones findings should prove to be incorrect / unjustified. Faith is different from knowledge that can be understood as a true and justified fact.

The religious belief (basic attitude of trust and also approving) is always based on the will / willing (the conversion of ideas into reality through actions) to believe and assumes the absolute truth of the belief content (e.g. the existence of god (god / good) ~ in the form of the good ...)

"religiousness" denotes the awe in front of the order and diversity in the world and the general sensation one transcendent independent reality (which lies outside / beyond the realm of possible (finite) experience and sensory perception, i.e. is not immanent), while "belief" means "be convinced" from the teaching of a specific religion (orphilosophy) includes.

(Wikipedia)

Many scholars regard belief in God as superstition because they have no evidence that God exists; it is an unrealistic clouding of consciousness that many believers are subject to. However, it has not been proven that god does not exist.

Many correct values are represented by religions (see also "table of goodness").

Spiritual values (which are symbolized by candlelight) represent something divine (wherever there is light, there is also life - that is a part of something good).

Believing in them is certainly good, but of course also in yourself as part of the whole. The individual spirit is important to diversity in a religious community.

<u>**Different religions:**</u> (Wikipedia)

- **Christianity (2.2 M):** Christianity is one World religion that from the Judaism (Suggestion: Add 10 commandments 2 to Moses: Don't be too selfish (11), golden rule (12)). Her followers are called Christians; the whole of Christians is also called Christianity. Central to Christianity is Jesus of Nazareth, a Jewish traveling preacher who appeared around AD 28-30 and in Jerusalem was executed. His younger recognized in him after his crucifixion and resurrection the son god and from Judaism expected messiah. They name him in their confessions Jesus Christ. Belief in him is in the scriptures of the New Testament basic.

- **Islam (1.5 M):** Islam is one monotheistic religion that began in the early 7th century ADArabia through the Meccans Mohammed donated has been. Islam is also commonly called Abrahamic, when prophetic revelation religion and as book or scripture religion designated. The Arabic word islām is a verbal no unto the Arabic verb "aslama" (surrender, surrender). It literally means "surrender" (into the will of God). The term for one who belongs to Islam is Muslim. The plural form in German is Muslims or Muslims, Muslims, Muslims.

- **Secularism (1.1 M):** (of Latinsaeculum 'time', age '; also: 'Century', as' this-sided 'contrast to the religious' other-sided' understood 'eternity') denotes a worldview that is based on the immanence and secularization the society limited and to further, metaphysical and religious no questions asked. It arises from two processes: On the one hand from the secularization, so the mental process of disentanglement or separation between religion and state, on the other hand from the secularization, the concrete process of replacing the secular power of religious institutions.

- **Hinduism (0.9 M):** Hinduism is also called Sanatana Dharma (the eternal law). It has its origin in India. Followers of Hinduism are called Hindus (from European-colonialist perspective). In contrast to other religions, there is no founder of religion in Hinduism, rather the religious systems of India developed over a period of approx. 3500 years. Hinduism therefore basically unites different religions, some of which overlap with common traditions and influence one another, but show differences in holy scriptures, beliefs, the world of gods and rituals. (Terms include "caste", "reincarnation").

- **Buddhism (0.38 M):** Buddhism is not theistic religion and so does not have the worship of an almighty God as its center. Rather, they relate beliefs of most Buddhist teachings on extensive philosophical-logical considerations as it is also in Chinese Daoismand Confucianism the case is. Therefore it is not revelation religion. What all Buddhists have in common is that they rely on the teachings of Siddhartha Gautama ("HistoricalBuddha") - the awakened called. What is meant is a fundamental and liberating insight into the basic facts of all life, from which the overcoming of the painful existence results. This knowledge can be attained by following his teachings in the form of Buddhist practice. The two extremes become more self-destructive as ceticism and unbridled hedonism, but also generally advised against radicalism, rather a middle way be taken.

- **Ethnic religions (0.27 M):** All orally or through rituals handed down belief systems that have not been fixed in writing to teach know. Followers only belong to one group.

<u>**Christianity:**</u>

"Christian faith is turning to christian god and correctly understood turning away from oneself. It is therefore seen as incompatible with self-fame and trust in one's own actions. What all Christian currents have in common is the belief that all that is through God was created and kept in existence.

At the center of this creation is the man who, however, is not capable of doing good on their own (original sin) and love and grace Jesus Christ needs to saved to become and eternal life to get. Jesus Christ is after Christian doctrine incarnate son of God.

The three persons of the Christian deity, God the son, God the father and God the Holy Spirit, aretriune.

The basis of faith is the holy scriptures bible that is seen as inspired by God.

A major point of contention among the Christian denominations has been sincere formation the question of whether man is justified before God by his faith alone, as in particular Martin Luther it has emphasized, or whether this also requires good works, because faith without works is dead, as it is underlined in Catholicism.

According to general Christian belief, belief is that personal answer to God's or Jesus' word. This answer always happens in the community of all believers and representativefor all humans. There is disagreement over the question of whether the full reality of faith takes place in the heart of the individual (so most evangelicalor protestant denominations) or whether the faith of the church ontological (metaphysical) priority (according to Catholic teaching).

The way of life shaped by the Christian faith is called piety designated."

(Wikipedia)

<u>**Reformation of the Church**</u>

According to a 2019 survey, the church would lose half of its members in the future (30 to 50 years) if it did not reform (which was then approved).

<u>Here are my suggestions:</u>

- Symbolism: The crucifixion of Jesus Christ only represents the sad end of the story, but not the main story, namely his speeches and his work in front of the population. So it should be placed at the center of the church altar.

- Design: Jesus drank from a wooden jug and spoke of helping poor people, it would be more authentic to make the churches natural and simple again: Good stone and wood material, light walls / no dark walls, no pompous building with gold leaf, just with colorful glass windows / lighting: colors illuminating the event (e.g. baptism)

- Comfort: Many people would certainly like to sit more comfortably in the church, which the uncomfortable (medieval) wooden benches do not allow -> furniture.

- Music: Spiritual music with not hypocritical phonetics and modern technology.

- A water dispenser, some bread and clothes (from the second warehouse) in the church to help thirsty, hungry and lumpy contemporaries.

- There should always be the possibility to call a clergyman with a bell or to speak / confess with one via the phone app.

- A theology student should take a minor in medicine to know ...

- Clergymen (pastors, nuns, monks) should absolutely adhere to the health and nutritional recommendations (in this book) regarding the "lust for meat" ...

- As an additional source of income, "the church" could rent its building once a month to an esoteric group for a (quiet & spiritual) event ...

<u>**School:**</u>

Before going to school, you should do a (mental and physical) health check on the little ones to check that they are fit for school and, if necessary, to resolve illnesses. At the beginning of school, there should then be an awareness of the importance of teaching and learning in life ...

In school you should learn the basic knowledge in different areas (subjects). In addition, the students should go to class regularly, where they should listen, learn to read and write, and also draw, sing and do gymnastics.

For further school it is highly recommended to teach the following subjects:

- "Health, exercise and nutrition" (so that there are fewer sick people)
- "Laws and justice" (so that there is less crime and prisons)
- "Money and finances" (so that there are fewer poor houses)
- "Philosophy" (optional)

The teacher should make the lessons as interesting as possible so that the students enjoy going to school and taking part there. Theories should be presented clearly and visualized using practical examples.... At the end of the lesson there should be enough time (10 min) so that the students can discuss the topic, which contributes to personal development, so that it is not just memorized ...

The students should practice what they have learned a little more at home ...

What has been learned should be checked regularly in order to bring a student to re-learn if necessary ... this requires a performance assessment system.

The following graphic illustrates such an assessment system, the idea being that performance is assessed as a percentage (how much % is correct of what the student has written) in order to compare (i.e. standardized) and award it everywhere (between different schools) accordingly the corresponding grade, whereby it should be noted that only the author of the content himself gets 100%:

<u>"Tabula rasa":</u>

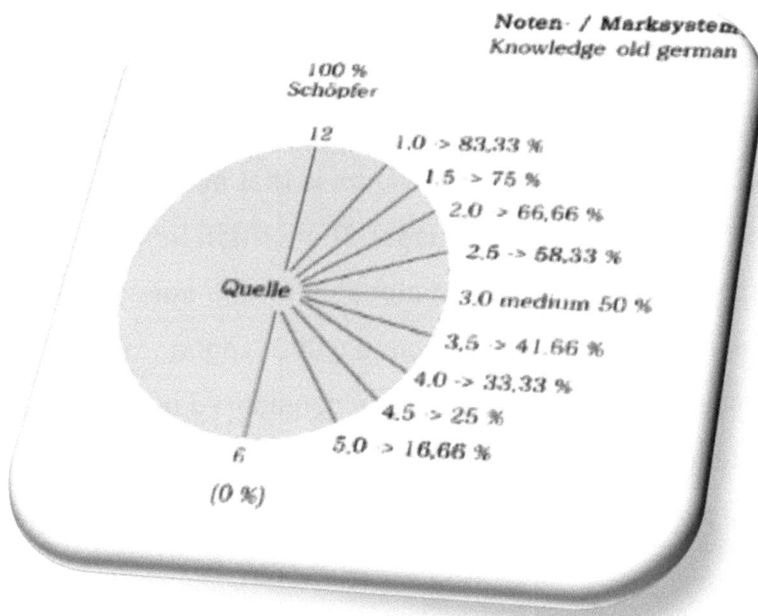

Example: For the evaluation of a spell check, you should possibly calculate how many letters a text has and how many of them have been spelled correctly. This evaluation principle is more understandable, especially for foreign students....

Tip: If one of the teachers does not like one, you should look for a new one....

Exercise idea: Since there are several countries (for example China and Israel) that write in a different direction than we Europeans, the teacher should try this spelling with the students:

Left-handed people could write from left to right.

Right-handed people could write from right to left.

(This may result in a correct combination between thinking and acting ...)

Language:

"In the general sense, language is understood to mean all complex systems of the communication. This includes the human ones natural languages and also constructed languages, but also in sign systems exist in the animal kingdom and communicative acts called language such as the dance language of bees. Among human natural languages, an essential division is that between spoken language and sign language (including body language). The written language is often an illustration of a spoken language (e.g. in alphabet fonts), but can also be independent of it (logography) ... there are around 6,000 languages worldwide ... currently the 50 most common languages are considered by around 80 percent of humanity mother tongue (and spoken by around 90% as a second language). The scientific discipline that deals with human language in general is linguistics. "(Wikipedia)

Language is an expression of human beings to communicate with others. The language is made up of tones, words and grammar. The phonetics, the size of the vocabulary, the choice of words and the sentence structure are decisive. The font, size and color also say something. The oral language can be used to identify gender, age, origin of the person, level of education and possibly also the profession. A common language is part of a people's culture. Anyone who wants to integrate into a people as a stranger should learn the language of this people. But a tourist should also be able to speak the national language (at least English).

A recommendation to learn foreign languages cheaply online: www.babbel.com

If there is a dialogue between, there is an exchange. In a discussion, a moderator is often helpful to steer the conversation ...

Tip: Talk to strangers about factual issues, with friends about private things.

Creative people like to "invent" new sounds and words, vary phonemes and morphemes, make special conjunctions, new corruptions or change the morphology – for example by drawing two nipples on the letter "B" ...

Art:

"The word art in the broadest sense denotes any developed activity that involves knowledge, exercise, perception, idea and intuition was founded ... since the time of enlightenment art is above all the form of expression of the fine arts:

- visual arts with the classic genera painting and graphic, sculpture, architecture, handicrafts, etc.
- music with the main divisions composition and interpretation in vocal- and instrumental music
- literature with the main genera epic, drama, poetry and essay writing
- performing arts with the main divisions theatre, dance and movie

Be practitioners of art in the narrower sense artists called. "(Wikipedia)

Art can be practiced in a variety of areas in different ways and speaks to people with their (individual) feelings – it can strengthen but also weaken them. Tolerance is the prerequisite for acceptance.

- You mostly "love" art that has a positive influence on you yourself.

- Diversity speaks to many different people (and is wealth).

- Art that inspires many (same) people is a mass phenomenon.

- Everything can be represented: chaos and order, reality and fiction.

- The higher quality the art, the better it is.

- There is something harmonious about the perfect geometry (of a sphere).

- Art can also be used politically and economically, among other things.

- Art can be a distraction or inspiration at work.

Note: Successful artists should help young talent (with money) ...

<u>**To shape:**</u>

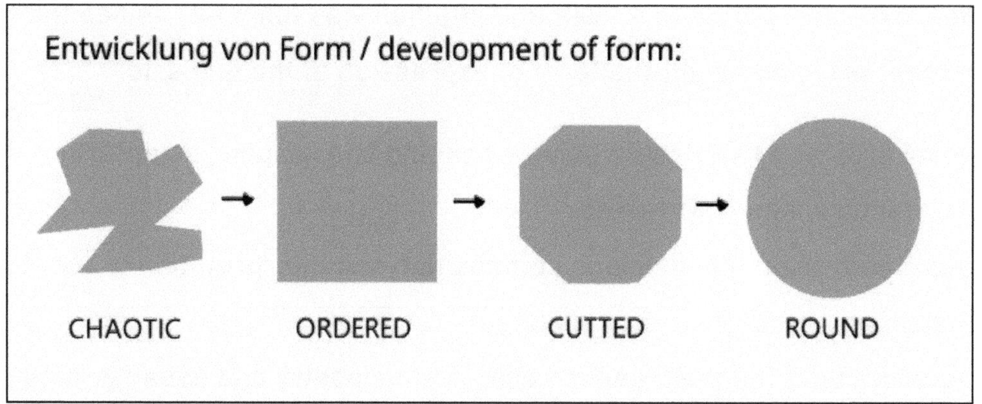

CHAOTIC: Asymmetrical, inharmonious, unbalanced, unstable

ORDERED: Straight, symmetrical, but angular and not round (inharmonious)

CUTTED: Like cubes, but less hard corners (more harmonious) ...

ROUND: Harmonious, symmetrical, stable – always balanced (in equilibrium), the same distance from the center to the edge = perfect shape in the geometry and thus the orientation in the center of the following graphic:

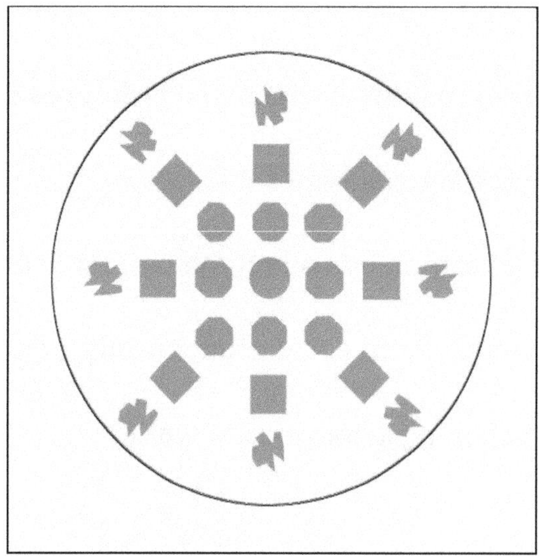

<u>Colours:</u>

"Color is a term that is used in very diverse ways in everyday life, in science and in art" (Wikipedia). Colors have certain meanings due to their connection to natural things, but also a mythological background * that these colors have from a "European point of view":

- white: Star = light, energy, life (-> mostly above*)
- yellow: Lemon = sour, vitalizing, refreshing
- green: Plants = growing, changing, shaping
- yellow-orange: Mandarin = fruity, sweet, rich in vitamins
- orange: Carrot, carrot = fiber, vitamin A (uge = in German: Eye)
- red: Fire, rose, blood = hot, romantic, binding (-> right *)
- purple, rose: Lilacs (butterflies), Eros / Cupid, grapes, UV
- blue: Water, sky = cool, refreshing, free (-> left *)
- dark blue: Deep sea = mysterious, flowing, drawing in
- black: Space, cave = dark, nothing, cold, dead (-> below *)

It is said that the color white contains all colors, but it is reasonable to assume that white light brings out all the colors of things.

Even if you can associate colors with things and they thus have certain meanings and contain certain feelings, you cannot generalize personal taste, as this is related to your own colors and preferences. Beauty is more a question of shape than color ...

Other forms of life sometimes see these colors differently. Artificial coloring is ignored here because it is based on arbitrariness; in addition, artificial colors can make you restless, natural colors are more calming (safer). If you give things the wrong color (e.g. books, videos, audios) it is like make-up or clothes that don't suit you - the reference ("context") is then wrong. Material color for wood, metal, stone, cement should also not alienate the awareness of the material, otherwise one lives in an untruth (lie) ...

<u>**Shapes and colors:**</u>

The world is richer when it is more diverse and therefore more colorful - and not monotonous and thus poor - but the claim to truth and order is there....

If you combine shape and color, the following cross-sectional graphic is created:

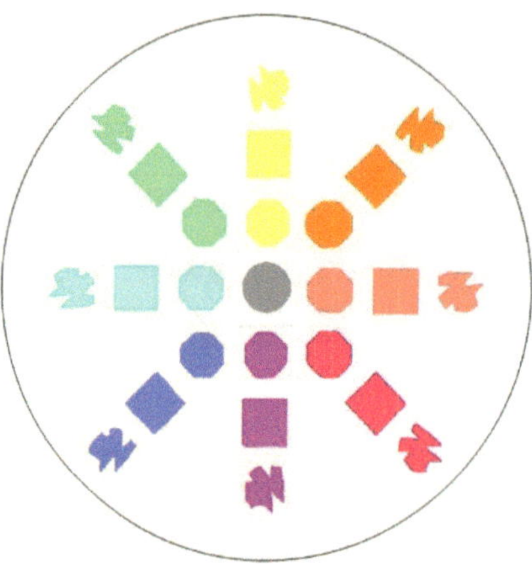

If you use the graphic above as a template for the Earth, you get the following map:

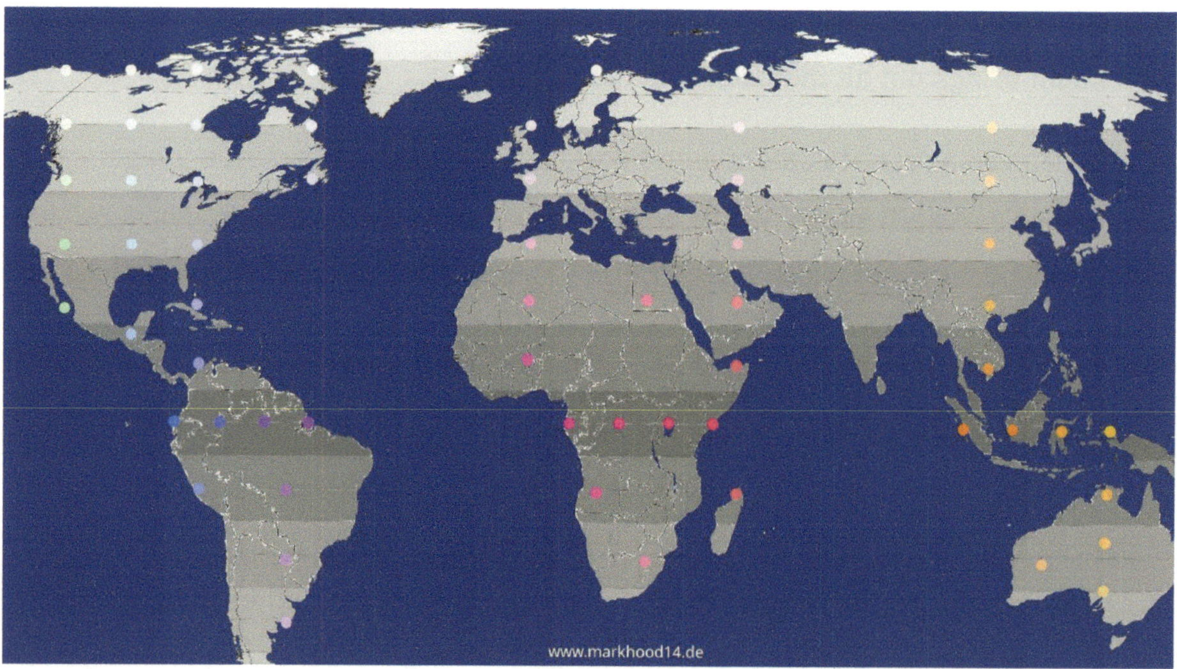

<u>**Music:**</u>

"Music is one art genre, their works consist of organized sound events. Becomes their creation acoustic material, such as tones, sounds and sounds, within the for people audible range, sorted. "(German Wikipedia)

The art is not only composing, but also singing / playing …

"From the supply one sound system will scales educated. Their tones can be of different volume or intensity (dynamics), timbre, pitch and sound duration appear. Melodies arise from the sequence of tones and possibly breaks within a fixed time frame (rhythm, meter and tempo, possibly embedded in bars). From the harmony of several tones (chords) grows from a different pitch polyphony, from the relationships of tones arises among each other harmony". (German Wikipedia)

"Among other things, music can also be viewed as a system of signs. Music can be intended meanings communicate with active, understanding listening. To this extent, listening represents a structuring process in which the listener iconic,indexical and symbolic drawing qualities differentiates and processes it cognitively. On the one hand, this is based on people's original experience of hearing and assigning sound events in visual form – e. g. thunder as a threatening natural event – and to reflect emotionally, on the other hand on the aesthetic appropriation of the acoustic environment. This ranges from the functionalization of the clay structures as signals to the symbolic transcendence of whole works" (German Wikipedia).

Beyond the canon of the musicological disciplines, music is the subject of research, e.g. in mathematics, communication science and medicine.

music = communication and "information"

"Music was often seen as a unity between dance, culture and language or as a unity of poetry, dance and musical art. At the turn of the 20th century, sound recording made the technical reproduction of music possible and increased the presence and availability of music enormously, especially through the mass media and then also through the digital revolution and the Internet. "(German Wikipedia)

<u>There are different styles of music:</u>

Flute music, birdsong, folk music, ritual music, cult ceremonies, secular music, instrumental music, traditional African music, choral music, romantic music, ballet music, children's music, film music, light music, dance and Salon music, operetta and musical, jazzmusic, popmusic, rock music, heavy metal, rap, reggae and tala, techno music, industrial, third stream, digital hardcore, crossover and world music.

You can listen to music on the radio for free and then buy a copy over the Internet for € 1 – music has to be paid for so that the musician can live off the income (or pay his costs). This is important…

In order to properly hear music, singing and noises, you have to Ear healthy (Check with an ear specialist / doctor !) and the audio technology be of good quality (you can measure that).

Mostly appealing is music whose content fits the current emotional situation of the respective listener. Alcohol and drugs can intensify music, but also the psych. and physical health damage accordingly …

You can hear your soul in your (own) voice – whether you are doing well in life.

"If you want to know who you are yourself, then listen to …" ☺

music can also be medicine (for the soul).

Music could be sent into space, the question probably not being if something comes back, but when … :-D

Annotation:

Music is very important for the mood and the soul, but not the main story. In the theater, the musicians sit in an orchestra pit between the auditorium and the stage – this structure makes sense accordingly.

<u>**Emotions:**</u>

Everyone has (individual and cultural) feelings / emotions and his / her action (which has to be mathematically and technically correct in order for it to work) is more or less influenced by them, which is basically of integrity, since they lead to something further emotional (see chapter philosophy). You can differentiate between good and bad emotions. Most of the time, positive emotions lead to positive ones and negative to negative ones. Feelings should be lived out in the right strength for the good of the soul (for example singing, happy or crying) and not "gnawing into" oneself in order to express them, to develop them, to get rid of (through expression), which is good for the voice (expression of soul) is ...

The following is a graphic (using Gauss' normal distribution approach) that is supposed to show the influence and course of feelings at the moment:

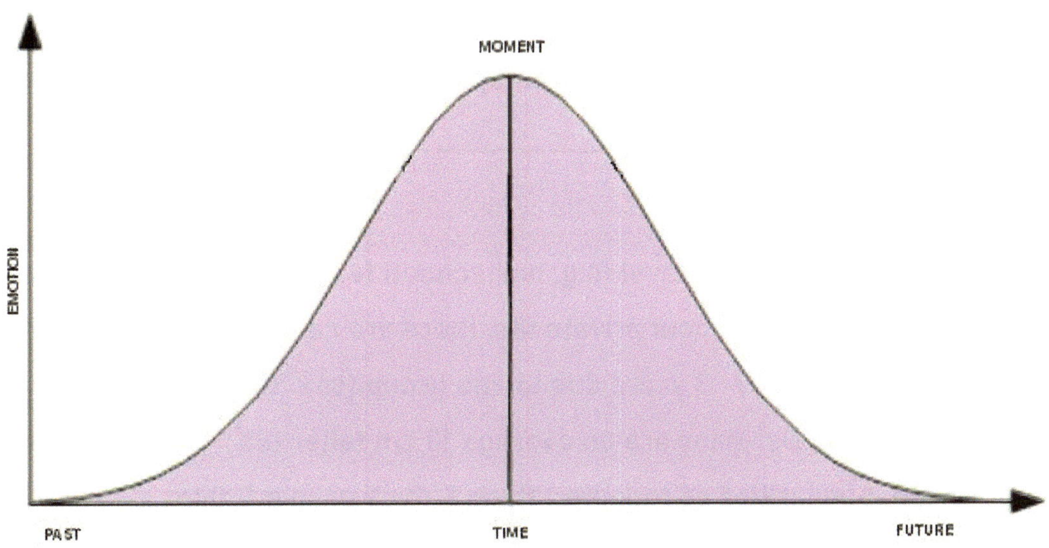

The time scale (x-axis) can be very different for people.

Note: The soul can also consist of a pair (e.g. femme + man) ... When you fall in love with the other person's voice, you love their soul too. (You can look different, unless you only know yourself.)

<u>**Partner choice:**</u>

Society is somewhat misguided by older generations who grew up at a time when there was a shortage of material things and women did not have the same income opportunities in the labor market as men. During this time, due to these factors, there were many partnerships and marriages in which the partners did not quite fit together, other things were more important during this time, such as financial security. In conclusion, one has tolerated adultery for fun. Meanwhile, women's incomes have improved somewhat, but are still lower than men's due to the difference in performance. Therefore it makes sense to get together (and to have a common fund), for example in the form of a community of gains, whereby the woman gives the man (beauty and love) feelings as a balance. Most of the time you have the same feelings with similar people that make you feel stronger, but then you may like something about a dissimilar person that you don't have yourself, but need in life. The feelings of the other can be recognized by their voice (= soul). The sympathy for one another should be equally strong (ie not one-sided) ... both should discuss at the beginning whether it is an open / tight bond ...

Matching criteria:

- Education: The same level (e.g. highschool) for the common conversation that should take place about private life, there are colleagues for professional life.
- Age: difference +/- 3 years due to age group (sex for him off 60 y: concubine)
- Size: men in Germany are on average 13 cm taller (8%) - it fits from the hips.
- Shape: Similarities go together: thick & thick or thin & thin
- Color: Same colors or different colors?

    a.) The same colors, if it is only about reproduction by the children, as they need an optical orientation (belonging) to the parents.

    b.) Different colors, if the partners want to achieve a color compensation: You balance yourself in color and are more competent ...

-> That means that you have several different partners in life.

<u>**Sex:**</u>

Sex is the prerequisite for the reproduction and survival of most living things, is healthy for the body and is fun for people. An initial change of partner can lead to the goal of finding the right - "equally" attractive - partner who one then might keep (because of desire). The sexual partners should agree spiritually, physically fit together in structure and shape (morphology) (a hand comparison helps, ~ 12% difference is normal) and fit together emotionally (you should also pay attention to the voice of the other, which reflects the feelings - maybe it should sound sexy). Unsuitable couples are usually dissatisfied, disoriented and grumble, a psychosomatic interaction. The position during sex also plays a role. If it works (mostly with men), the woman also gets an "orgasm" (no allure because of a more beautiful one), which affects the affection for the man. In the man this is evidently through ejaculation, in the woman through relaxation and a vocal tone, which could be related to the fact that the feeling tells you "to have found the right one", which of the mechanics of the woman's anatomy is related to could have done - around the 14th day of the cycle - so that the egg then slides through the fallopian tube to the center to mix with the sperm for a baby. The woman's internal clock and blood pressure are also correct. The woman is then nice, content and calmer. In addition, androgens (in men) or estrogens (in women) are then "influenced", which leads to that new sperm is produced in men (with the side effect of muscle doping) and milk production is stimulated in women (for the baby) - which makes the breasts look a little plumper and more beautiful after a while. The two then look more attractive after a while. You don't need to be ashamed of it - the lives of people who have found the right partner can be extended by several years (especially with men). The place, the environment (and the lighting) can also have a great effect on the pairing behavior, stimulating means such as food and drink (including as an aphro-disiac), clothing and certain "toys" have a supportive effect. You should find the middle between pleasure and asceticism (Buddhist approach) during sex ...

Statistics: In the south, sex every 3 days (like in sport) has proven itself to be in a good mood, but at least once a week to maintain the current state.

If a man is only interested in his own climax (which is the case in many relationships), he should pay the woman money (gifts) for it (as in a brothel):

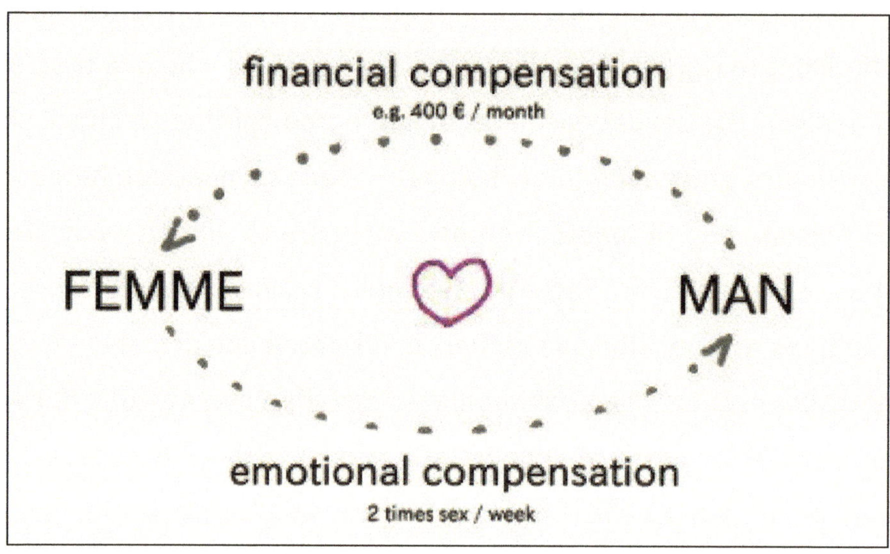

The € 400 a month makes a lot for women who earn little / mediocre money; she
can afford more in life -> gym, better cosmetics, nutrition, clothes and shoes, he can
say that he does sex for relaxation after work (normal, but not natural) ...

P.S. Private sex is actually none of your business as long as it doesn't happen there
- snoopers and suspenders have no place in other people's love lives. However,
there are also places for extroverted people, such as swinger clubs, to "present"
themselves. Men should behave like a gentleman towards women when it comes to
sex - and not tell other men a lot about it, because the woman may be
uncomfortable because of her "image" (because of the shame caused by the
anatomy, but also by the views and words of church, parental home and partly
society). People who perceive sex as "dirty" (also because of unclean incidents with
spit, urine, feces, blood and dirt) have an unnatural understanding of sex - they
often say "dirty stuff" about it, but confuse their own overeating with pork
(especially with sausage and ham) emotionally with it (because this can make you
more instinctive due to the hormones it contains). Certain perversions have
intensified this talk. Oral and anal intercourse can be criticized, but gays (who often
do an excellent job) and lesbians (who have had enough of men) have no other
option to have sex with their partner. Pedophiles, necrophilia, sodomites and
inbreeding fans are "sick" and should perhaps (have to) consult a psychologist or
psychiatrist...

<u>**Health:**</u>

Health is the basis of being and should always come first. **A healthy long life seems to be the most beneficial**. How old you get depends not only on your own genetics, but also on "epigenetics" (including your own behavior and that of your partner) - therefore the topic "take care of your health should be taught in school through information and education: Oxygen (air), drinking and eating (nutrition), exercise (15min walking a day or 2 times sport a week), gentle work, restful sleep in a closed quiet room - in a warm, good bed (plate slatted frame, cold foam mattress (~25cm), anti-mite cover), danger avoidance (p. 31), good and safe living environment (house in nature in a constitutional state), sunny and rainy days (climate), good sitting posture on a solid, comfortable and appropriately chair (because of the back and the hip), doctors nearby, as well as hygiene, care and pharmaceuticals, the right loyal partner for emotions, sex and children (p. 20-22), transport routes to / from supply stores, comfortable clothing, keeping ideal weight (BMI + 10 %), since overweight leads to stress and damage and underweight leads to an weakness and insecurity. Avoid harmful consumer good (alcohol, cigarettes, drugs, too much fat and (bad) meat). Additionally sauna (1 x month) to clean the derma (the scin organ), take an (individual) multivitamin tablet once a week to support the supply of vitamins and nutrients, as well as regular health examinations and test. You can do something for feelings and well-being of your soul with your partner, with friends, in a club / association, group, community, with animal and with media (movies, radio, games). It is very important to have a balance between left and right (through learned dual thinking) that is practised in movement (Buddhist way) like joint-friendly back swimming exercises (back-strokes) in a lake or swimming pool. Don´t forget to have money for everything…

<u>**Nutrition:**</u>

Eating and drinking is very important for health, feelings (soul) and the performance of the body. You can make a lot of yourself in connection with work and sport. "Do everything yourself" - that means you are responsible for your own nutrition...

Eating too little leads to weakness, and eating too much leads to excess with associated disadvantages. You can use the BMI (Internet calculator) to determine your ideal weight, taking age, height, weight (and gender) into account. If you want a little more security in the form of a reserve (for winter, bad times, illness), you can add 10%.

In principle one could (in prison) "feed on (pure) water and (fresh) bread" - but since human beings consist of 80 percent water, to "flush" the body (with nutrients) it should also take **2 –Drink 3 liters of water**, but the main components of the diet should be **proteins, carbohydrates and fats** (especially for children in sterile, healthy milk - the quality regulation and control should be improved!). Humans also need **roughage (salad), herbs (tea), trace elements (iodine), vitamins (juice), minerals and spices (against parasites)**. The German Society for Nutrition gives approaches as to how much a person needs of something every day, but this should again be considered individually. A doctor can also use a blood test to determine which components are lacking in the body or where there is an excess. Desirable is a (EDP) nutrition program for the home, where you can make individual entries...

Meat: "You are what you eat" - are the eaten animals now your soul? (Dr Moreau)

You can tell what you eat by looking at your teeth - compared to other creatures (herbivores and carnivores), especially their closest relatives, the monkeys. Most monkeys are herbivores, but there are some carnivores, identified by their sharp teeth designed to tear flesh. For humans (4 canines of 32 teeth) the **7/8 diet** is made up of **salad** (to stimulate intestinal peristalsis) and then **pasta** (with carbohydrates for energy and 13% protein for the muscles) and **1/8 meat** (200g non-toxic) a week quality steamed beef (for muscles and vitamin B12 (which can be stored in the body) against blood anemia). Of course, too much beef can lead to colon cancer in normal people, and pork (including sausage and ham) can cause inflammation and rheumatism due to the arachidonic acid It is better to eat a chicken and every 1-2 weeks fish (saithe) or shrimp to provide the omega-3 fatty acids (only the animals have it ready) for the cell membranes

<u>Weekly nutrition plan:</u>

Breakfast:	Having lunch:	Dinner:
Oatmeal, apple, honey	Bucatini with tomato sauce (garlic)	Cheese bread + tomato
Toast with jam, nut	Vegetable soup with chicken	„Brezel" + butter
Yogurt with fruits	Pizza Margherita	Baguette with cheese 2
Oatmeal, apple, honey	Farfalle with 100g salmon (white wine)	Cheese bread + tomato
Toast with jam, nut	Dalmatian ham with olives, cucumber	„Brezel" + butter
Yogurt with fruits	Tagliatelle with mushrooms	Baguette with cheese 2
Oatmeal, apple, honey	200g rump steak, rice (red wine)	Cheese bread + tomato

<u>Preparation:</u>

During the preparation one should try to cook (heating in the moist state: steam sterilization) in order to kill germs, bacteria, worms, etc. that may be in the raw food. Roasting is dangerous because burned food can cause cancer. It is best to "bake" (heating for hours in a dry state: hot air sterilization) in the oven:

- Pathogenic streptococci, listeria and polioviruses are killed at 61.5 ° C in 30 minutes.

- Most vegetative bacteria, yeasts, molds, all viruses except hepatitis B are killed at 80 ° C in 30 minutes

- Hepatitis B viruses, most fungal spores are killed at 100 ° C in 5-30 minutes (some above)

- Prions (deadly cousins of our protein molecules -> with BSE) are killed at 132 ° C in 60 minutes.

By killing these pathogens through sterilization you protect your life (from death) …

<u>Enjoy the meal:</u> It is important to chew the food enough so that it is nicely chopped up and crushed, which makes it easier to absorb in the stomach and intestines. Digestif helps. After eating clean your mouth: toothpaste, toothbrush and mouthwash. Bad breath often suggests wrong and / or bad food …

<u>Hygiene:</u> An important component of hygiene is washing dishes and disposing of food waste (in the garbage can), as these often attract pests due to the smell. The toilet should also be cleaned and have an appropriately large seat, as this is much more relaxing during the "discharge"

<u>**Sports:**</u>

Sport sounds very strenuous at first, such as "sprint", but it is very important for health. The anatomical movement promotes blood circulation and stimulates the body to build muscles; joints are also "lubricated". You also get a nice shape and become more attractive. Movement is a sign of life. One can visualize one's fuel (balance) and one's soul (feelings) through movement, practically depict them and demonstrate the unity between spirit, soul and body and perhaps receive praise from others for what affects the mind - a confirmation that it has been done correctly that creates security and possibly respect. The action in sport should be logical in order to achieve the goal, but the implementation in the movement should be done with feeling, ie dynamic (appropriate), sliding, round and harmonious....

Exercise and sport are particularly important for adolescents, as they significantly shape their later form, but are also important for middle age in order to have the strength, endurance and speed to cope with life, but also for older people to stay fit - When exercising, the "work" counts for a long time....

1 x week sport serves to maintain performance, more to increase it....

You should build up the muscles through sport in order to be able to move your own body weight optimally, less leads to inability to act, more to exaggeration with corresponding disadvantages in other areas (speed). Therefore always train with your own weight, which is perfect for everyone - overpressure on joints and cartilage (through weights) should be avoided.

Anyone doing sport stimulates the body to adapt to the activity. What you do there depends on your preference, but the whole body should always be trained in side-sync and the areas (speed, strength and endurance) balanced. "No price without sweat" - a lot is removed from the body through movement if you do not go to the sauna. Movement probably makes the ferrite "glow" in the blood. In order to build up, the body needs appropriate substances (through eating and drinking). Exercise is the best "fat burner" because fat is superfluous weight and leads to increased stress on the body (joints, heart), even if a small reserve is a security (for the winter). Excess, injuries, doping and overexertion should be avoided. Magnesium and warm baths help with sore muscles. In the event of injuries, you should first cool with a gel and apply a warming ointment after 3 days to promote blood circulation.

Posture bands are also often helpful for support. In sport, the right equipment, especially shoes, is very important for the result and success. Team sports promote the ideal of team play. Meditation can lead to internalization of the movement associated with the sport. One could also use a computer-based training program with an anonymous connection to a large database on the Internet and an interface to a health and nutrition program. The doctor could also take a small sample of meat from the body to check the consistency of the tissue ...

<u>Graphics for the sauna:</u>

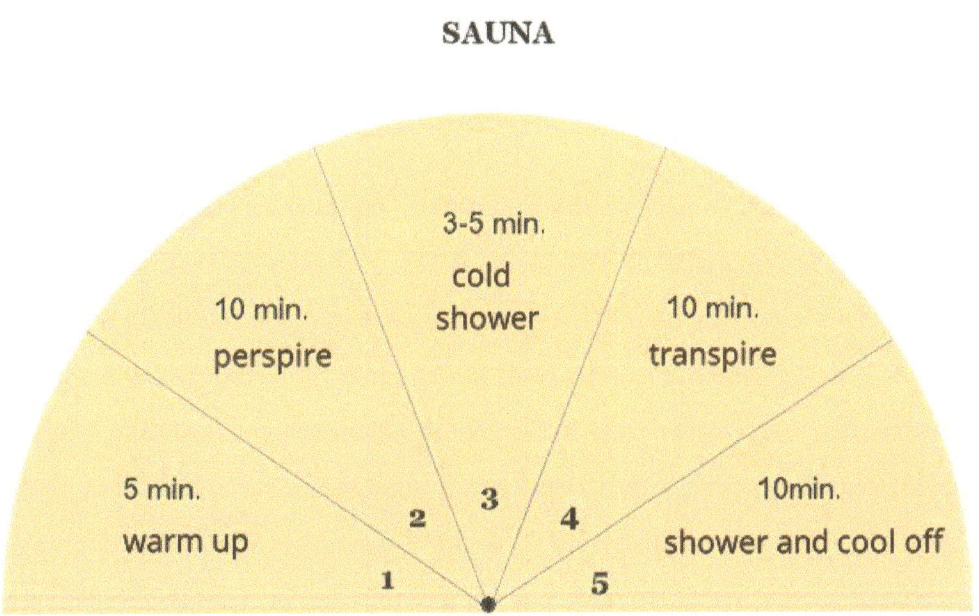

at least once a month

Medicine:

Medicine is an important component of health and treats diseases as an afterthought. But also disease prevention (prophylaxis) should be a component in society (quasi as a precaution (see chapter health)) through education …

Medicine was available in most countries on every continent. In Europe white medicine, with the Indians the medicine man, with the Asians e.g. Chinese medicine and with the Arabs medicine very early (compare the book "The Medicus"). Religions often hindered medicine in the past, but science changed this. In the meantime, modern (computer) technology can be used in medicine and the internet enables a worldwide exchange of medical knowledge. Empirical surveys, statistics and warnings, especially from well-known institutes (such as the German Robert Koch Institute), are important for medicine. Although these are currently always very important, people often do not live healthier either, which is an educational problem, the job of the government is - "How will I be 100 years old" could be the name of the new school subject. A small medical degree (2 years) would be good (for theologians as a minor).

In medicine, it is important to provide the patient with the perfect treatment: First, the patient is recorded by the doctor as an individual with all personal characteristics and the data (encrypted in a "cloud" or on a "stick") is made available to a medical colleague made; if he feels unwell, you can find out exactly what the cause (s) is and possibly diagnose an illness. Then one decides whether it is to be treated with medicine (here too, one chooses the medicine (possibly from an international pharmacy) that is most suitable and that best addresses "the" patient in an appropriate dose over a period of time) or through a person comes (specialist doctor who is suitable and trained for this) or. The whole thing must also be paid for - health insurance contributions could be reduced through prevention. Even if it seems regrettable that large (pharmaceutical) companies tend to be profit-oriented, one can bear in mind that high research and development costs have to be amortized again. Donations from these companies to medical universities would be "nice" …

Hospital (and rehab): The room design should "help" psychosomatically - by using natural material (wood, stone) with a transparent protective layer (eg lacquer) for later sterilization. Fresh air, bed linen, clothes, and shower are all good.

"Open" medical findings and questions:

- The doctor should live theory in his own practice (for example, look healthy himself).

- Differences between genetically and socially (culturally) caused diseases …

- The word "antibody" seems to be a wrong term (compare with matter - antimatter).

- Are there better computer programs for patient data? Are all laboratory values standardized?

- New DNA analyzes and data -> individual medicines, blood and transplants.

- An international (European) pharmacy would be a treasure trove / gain in resources.

- Is it possible to extend life with preserved ("cold-put") own hormones?

- Surgery: Only people with fine hands should be allowed to work there …

- Women shouldn't have their breasts operated on while they need it for breastfeeding.

- Cancer is often caused by damaged cells from burned food (food, skin, cigarettes, etc.) …

- Neurology: What can "annoy" you …? (E.g. a broken tooth can be the reason) :-D

- Mentally ill through hearing (through shouting, blaring, interference (portable radio)) -> voice …

- Psychosomatic illnesses: e.g. tension due to wrong "values" (attitude)

- F00 * Alzheimer's (dementia): psychosomatic forgetting <- Therapy: Biography in retirement.

- F01 Binswanger (infarction): (cholesterine + fat) switch off source + solvent (pomegranate).

- F02* Parkinson: The simple logical treatment is Levodopa (L-Dopa), but the more intelligent option

  might be a blood transfusion from the son to refresh the genetic Material.

- F02 * Creuzfeldt-Jacok.: How prions apply their structure to our proteins for cloning …?

- F20 Schizophrenia: Discuss and clarify controversial past events from one's biography.

- F30-F40 Affective disorders come from the consumption of (pink / red) meat + heat.

- F60-F69: Personality / developmental disorders: reasons (parental home, environment) change …

- "How does a vestibular problem (in the semicircular canal, macular organs) lead to" dizziness "…?"

- Players often have a "Cavuum Vergae" - like little children … did they stay behind?

- A complete virus scan provides information about the possible causes of many diseases …

- In-depth research (biology, strategy, etc.) of the 9,000 virusfamilies -> prevention & medication.

- CMV has already been found in prostate cancer tissue -> CMV in semen -> sextherapy (+ condom).

- Alcohol works very well for germ disinfection after eating / sex / going out …

- Is a regular (every 3-5 years) germ cure with antibiotics (e.g. penicillin) not useful?

- Some patients have parasites (especially from vacation abroad) as the cause of the disease.

- The population should "regularly" eat raw German „Sauerkraut" against tapeworms …

- Marijuana / hemp can be used as a poison against parasites (and their diseases).

- Implants + foreign bodies are disruptive factors for the intuition / feeling, the senses!

- In case of damage to bones, cartilage, joints and ligaments -> reduce (over) weight.

- Prostheses and orthopedic shoe insoles are often firm and do not adapt to the changing shape in motion -> accidents! Solution: Hard rubber with cushioning.

- Rascals often mistreat people in the healing area (e.g. a massage without sensitivity).

- Antioxidants ("versus. H2O") to slow down the chemical reaction (with e_) as cell protection (please check selenium deficiency) or simply make sure that the drinking water is very good / clean ...?

- Dark circles under the eyes indicate poisoning (from food) and organ damage <- vitamins

- Illnesses caused by poisoning or lack of nutrients can be eliminated with a cure (3 months).

- Vitamins are disease prophylaxis (and against "rings"), why doesn't she pay the cash register?

- Are synthetic vitamins as effective as natural (with minor components)?

- Vitamin deficiencies can lead to illness - Why Not Have a regular checkup of these?

You should take 1-2 multivitamin tablets / week regularly, for example: www.centrum.at

Vitamins + (essential) fatty acids + iodine + milk:

A1	Retinol	S	Eyesight, cell growth, skin
B1	Thiamine	N	Carbohydrate metabolism, thyroid function, nerves
B2	Riboflavin	N	against migraines, promotes memory and concentration
B3	niacin	N	Recovery v. Fats, protein and carbohydrates, skin + nails
B5	Pantothenic acid	N	Wound healing, defense reaction
B6	Pyridoxine	N	Nerve protection, protein metabolism
B7	Biotin	N	Protection against skin inflammation, good forskin, Hair andNails
B9	Folic acid	N	good for the skin
B12	Cobalamin	S	forms and regeneratesRed blood cells, Appetite, nerves
C.	Ascorbic acid	N	Protection against infections, radical scavengers, for the connective tissue
D3	Cholecalciferol	S	Photo protection against skin cancer, calcium level
E.	Tocopherol	S	Cell renewal, inflammation, immune system, radical scavengers
F.	Omega fatty acids	S	Cell membrane, Skin, water balance, heart + vessels, etc.
K	Phylloquinone	N	Formation ofBlood clotting factors, Synthesis ofOsteocalcin
I.	Iodine / iot	S	Production of thyroid hormones (againstGoiter formation)
"M"	milk	?	Cell structure, against osteoporosis, high blood pressure, heart attack

S means, that vitamin, substance or element is stored, N means that it is not stored - in the body

(Source: Wikipedia)

<u>**Hazards:**</u>

"You only live once", after that you are dead forever. Therefore, everyone should try to live as long as possible by avoiding the following dangers:

- Injuries (physical, mental, emotional) by yourself or others
- Diseases (heart attacks, strokes, cancer, etc.)
- Biological hazards (bacteria, viruses, etc.)
- Consumer goods (alcohol, drugs, cigarettes, meat + fats, sugar)
- Spoiled food (see expiry date + origin)
- Poverty (no money for accommodation, food, medicine, clothing)
- Accidents: In traffic (bicycle, motorcycle, car, truck, ship, train, plane, helicopter) and sports (climbing, fighting, football, riding, etc.)
- Other people (violence, wars, murders, bodily harm, theft, robbery, rape, kidnapping, abuse, other crimes)
- Wrong political system (dictatorship or communism), wrong laws and injustice, violation of human rights, dangerous religions
- Own mistakes (criminal offenses, ignorance, wrong actions, debts)
- Dangerous animals (big cats, hyenas, wolves, bears, buffalo, crocodiles, fish (sharks), snakes, spiders, scorpions, insects, parasites, etc.)
- Poisonous plants (hemlock, monkshood, deadly nightshade, ricin)
- Natural disasters (earthquakes, tsunamis, tornadoes, hurricanes, thunderstorms, floods, volcanic eruptions, fires).
- Risk areas: Deserts (dying of thirst), sea (drowning), mountains (falling down), ice (freezing to death), volcano (burning up), space (suffocating), sky (falling)
- Radioactivity (radiation from nuclear power plants and X-rays)
- Chemicals (burns) + vapors (lung damage)
- Explosions (gas, gasoline, chemicals)
- Space (celestial bodies, black holes, supernovas, implosions)
- Hostile aliens (these would probably die of smallpox or something on Earth).

<u>**Alcohol:**</u>

Alcohol is an admixture / distillation and fermentation product in connection with another substance (e.g. grapes, herbs, malt) that gives the taste.

When it comes to alcohol, it always depends on how much man (m) or woman (f) drinks from the mixture that contains a certain alcohol level. The difference between the sexes is important because women weigh less and their water balance is different than that of men. Women tolerate much less …

Alcohol can have positive effects in limited quantities: One becomes more sociable, open, relaxed, more talkative and can sleep better at night - alcohol is sometimes also good for the stomach (kills bacteria, etc.) at certain meals:

1 (f) - 2 (m) alcohol. Drink (e.g. Prosecco) as an aperitif (Romanesque tradition)

1 (f) - 2 (m) glasses of white wine with fish, lobster and lobster (white meat)

1 (f) - 2 (m) glasses of red wine with beef fillet or steak (red meat)

1/3 liter (f) - 2/3 liter (m) of beer with roast pork, white sausages & pretzels

1 (f) - 2 (m) herbal liqueur (e.g. Averna) as a digestif after the Italian pasta meal

You can also talk to your doctor about how much alcohol you can tolerate personally and what damage alcohol does to the body (e.g. to the liver - treatment with artichoke. However, liver cirrhosis is fatal without a transplant).

More alcohol can lead to loss of control, you start to babble, you kiss strangers, smell of alcohol, walk curvy, babble at people, can no longer hold back with secrets, are "played out" by experienced races and are in a high-spirited state, in which unfortunately many still drive cars and some drive themselves dead. In a country where alcohol consumption is part of the culture, this happens quite often. To avoid this, you should definitely have organized a trip home beforehand or not even go to a pub / bar.

Cigarettes:

Cigarette consumption usually begins with the first cigarette (from a friend) which is immediately addictive (through nicotine and additives), which is underestimated by most. A cigarette in itself doesn't matter, but if you become addicted to one and then keep picking up on one, the whole thing will pile up over time: You will smoke 100,000 cigarettes over many years, get bad skin, breathing and lung problems, maybe at some point even lung cancer. Smoking the paper is also harmful, so some use a "vaporizer".

In the meantime, doctors differentiate between (+10) different types of lung cancer and there are various new (genetic) healing methods for this at famous (university) clinics, which are also paid for by certain health insurance companies.

But the money is also serious if you add up the costs for cigarettes over 20-30 years and come to +30,000 € - for this you could have bought a (middle-class) car, for example - it should also be mentioned that the The state levies taxes on every finished pack of cigarettes and also on every finished cigarette (a total of + 70% of the costs). Then it is cheaper to stuff yourself: with tubes in a mega-pack from the Internet, fresh tobacco in a packed, closed bag and a stuffing machine).

In order to get rid of cigarette consumption (addiction), you need a very strong will. There are supportive books, seminars, therapies (and a state telephone hotline), but if you don't feel like smoking one again, forget about quitting. Don't even start smoking!

What's good for smoking?

Lots of oxygen in the house (through plants, fresh air from outside), sauna, yoga, walking / jogging, vitamin C (fruits, vegetables), possibly acupuncture, nicotine patches or receptor block tablets (on prescription). Isn't there a remedy that you put into tobacco for over 1 year that you get apathy against smoking?

<u>**Drugs:**</u>

Drugs are very different (like medication), they can hardly be summed up in one word. People who are not (personally) familiar with drugs do not know (emotionally) what they are talking about - they have only heard about them - you could then also say that the following substances are drugs: dopamine, heroin, cocaine, amphetamine, coffeine, nicotine, saccharine. Some say that drugs make you lose touch with reality by putting you in a different / better (emotional) state for a certain period of time. But only as long as the effect lasts, then you feel worse and you want to go back to the previous "better" state by taking drugs again (etc.).

My personal experiences with drugs are:

- It's fun to smoke "weed" with students and talk about studying ...
- With the help of "dope & shit" you can really "talk shit" ...
- With cocaine you are "clear", the stamina is great and you feel "divine" ...
- "At speed" the cycle begins to race and everything is done quickly ...
- MDMA is great under the stars - this should be (legal) on wedding night.
- LSD causes unreal visions of faces and objects (to music) ...
- Heroin causes an immense emotional and colorful "twisting" (to music).

Many drugs are (here) illegal, but you also have the right to a certain amount for your own use - you can say for "work relaxation". The amount is regulated differently in each federal state. It is very unfortunate that the personal consumption of drugs cannot be bought in the pharmacy (as in Canada), but that they are traded on the black market, where there are always harmful admixtures that make you sick even though the doctor calls drugs "medicine" may prescribe against certain diseases. Indians from South America eat a naturally grown leaf of the coca plant ("bract") during the day to stimulate and revitalize, which fat people would do well to move more. Perhaps for this reason you should create the opportunity to legally buy this in the pharmacy (for 1 euro) every day.

Nevertheless, I would never take (hard) drugs again, as this meant that I could no longer "manage" my "normal" life (studies, work, income, girlfriend and family) - rarely maybe 1 joint of grass in my private room smoke…

<u>**Politics:**</u>

Politics used to be based on kings, emperors, tsars and rulers and represented a monarchy from which actually only the rulers really benefited and the people felt badly. Later the republic was proclaimed, the monarchy became a constitutional one, but dictatorships and fascism followed until a real **democratic system** emerged after its fall – with several parties that are also based on a basic law (a constitution). The principle behind this is to satisfy the feelings of the majority, who usually also win (e.g. a war). This was followed by the discussion about the distribution of money: communists wanted everyone to have the same amount of money and capitalists wanted only the successful people to have the money. Both principles still exist. An interim solution is the **free social market economy** in which monopolies are forbidden and employees are insured. Every people has the opportunity to elect (new) representatives to the government every few years, which changes again and again in order to create a balance through balancing. These representatives are mostly intellectually well-versed, can speak and negotiate very well (also with foreign countries). The freedom of expression and freedom of the press (according to the constitution) should guarantee that the people are not lied to or that information is not censored (as it used to be). Because politicians can negotiate so well, diplomacy is guaranteed, which prevents war in crisis situations, which is important!

My idea is to improve this democracy even further – to an **"optimized democracy"** in which every voter's vote is weighted with a personal "score". Maybe you could start by assigning scores to politicians. (and show the score).

But how do you judge each individual voter? "A music star can hear how much the vote (the voter's soul) counts…" The IQ of the voter is just as important: 1.2 times with an IQ of 120. Likewise the opinion to health (= ~life expectancy of the person). Following formula:

Total score = 1/3 soul (= voice) + 1/3 spirit (= IQ) + 1/3 body (= ~life expectancy)

The assessment of voice, mind and body should be made by a neutral (sound) institute. Voters should have the opportunity to improve their score.

There are risks (classification, outing) with this idea, you have to test it locally first

For reasons of fairness, disabled people should always get an average score.

<u>**Law:**</u>

The laws are made by representatives of the people, with the system being **based on a basic law** (constitution). After all, **"all people (from a legal point of view) are to be treated equally"** (to be treated), even if the court sees the **individual** case - unfortunately these views are sometimes naive, expensive lawyers (of celebrities) usually achieve a better result, judges have already decided in advance worked for the state. This means that judgments are usually influenced by national feelings. Sometimes some politicians lack integrity – falsehood, hypocrisy and corruption are tolerated for the benefit of the country, which has a bad effect on the behavior of the population and culture. It also seems that MPs have got a "bird" in their parliament. In (criminal) law, **mathematics should serve as a guideline** because it is universal, i.e. it is correct on every planet / in every place. This means, for example, that if someone committed a crime for 5 minutes, they should only receive a 5-minute punishment (to the same extent) so that there is a time equation. Theoretically, you always do to the perpetrator the same thing that he did himself: "Quitt pro quo", although you have to take into account that the victim (who would be entitled to do this) is a different person and cannot do the same thing himself – the intermediate question is: "Who is who?" and how is it "Net"? It is therefore incumbent on the judge (and the correctional officers) to create a parable, which is currently (transcendentally) not the case - even a sentence that is too high is a crime and should be punished (to the same mathematical extent). It is of course good that **lawyers have qualifications in the field. The judiciary is there to ensure that not every (unsuitable) layperson plays the role of judge** and executioner. A judge must make a neutral decision and should be able to assess the punishment based on personal experience (as an inmate). Perhaps a jury could also be appointed. Another idea is that the perpetrator can choose a punishment himself, which also depends on the crime (relative fine for financial crimes, immediate punishment for momentary damage, long prison sentence for longer-term damage). I would also like to point out that the term "lawyer" sounds illogical when it comes to a left-wing lawyer…

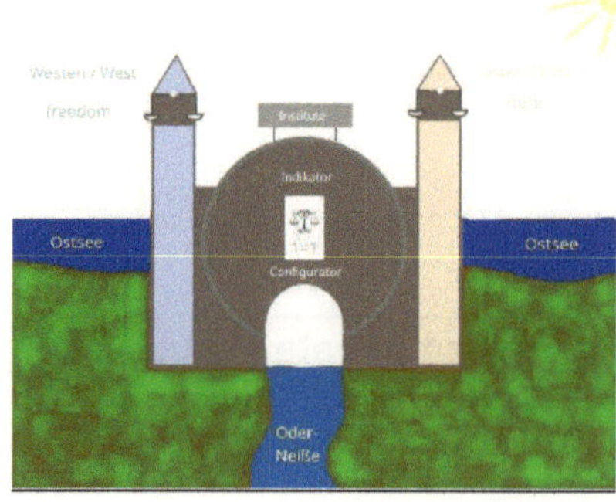

<u>"Legal Loopholes"</u>

Note: The German law is incomplete – "people have shamelessly exploited loopholes" (Chancellor A. Merkel in the 2018 election) + suggestions for improvement:

- In the case of penalties and statutes of limitations, the math should be correct (1 = 1)!
- Anyone who violates the Basic Law commits a criminal offense (should be § 1).
- State laws should not violate international law (UN).
- In the case of a crime, the jurisdiction of the court at the place of the crime always applies.
- In between speeches disturbs people's concentration and leads to mistakes.
- Lies are not honest and therefore an insult to honor (cf. 10 commandments).
- Women (~ who often lie) should be checked for their suitability for legal teaching.
- Deceptions (deception of reality) are misleading and transfigure the mind.
- Blackening, sneaking, betrayal and deceit are bad acts.
- Stalking could be punished as long as the person was stalking…
- Intrigues are intellectual machinations that cause harm to others.
- Oppression and displacement is interference in the honest process.
- Tricks are technical machinations that can harm others.
- Shit (by pushing, pebbles in the shoe) falsifies results.
- Provocations should be classified, prohibited and reprimanded (as an administrative offense).
- A woman's request for a condom during sex should be her women's right.
- Motivation to commit crimes by sexual intercourse could be classified as incitement.
- Infidelity should be punished by infidelity (possibility must exist legally).
- Cuckoo eggs and female theft destroy the bloodline / dynasty of a family.
- Witchcraft (with sex) should be punished (by an exorcist from the Church).
- Sexual abuse (of children) lead to sex. psych. disturbances (ICD 10, Chapter 5, F: 52, 64, 66) of the victims over a long period of time, should be compensated for a correspondingly long period (1 = 1).
- Affect offenses due to excessive meat consumption should be found out (cf. ICD 10, Chapter 5, F30-39).
- It is wrong to be allowed "puppets" (with dictatorship) doing crimes and punish just them.
- A criminal case is only understandable if the act matches the perpetrator … (clarification!)
- If a case happened because of a mistake, the perpetrator should go to the madhouse.
- If a case happens due to a disability, the perpetrator should go to a home of disabilied people.
- Taking revenge is wrong, demanding vengeance is right (must be taken into account).
- If the attempted murder failed, the perpetrator could be marked with an "M".
- A murderer should have a photo of the corpse in his (prison) room for the rest of his life…

According to the principle of legality, the police, customs, public prosecutors and tax investigator are obliged to investigate if they have knowledge of a criminal offense (abroad).

<u>**Violence:**</u>

"As violence (from „Old High German word „waltan" (be strong, master). Actions, operations and social contexts in which or through which on people, animals or objects has an influencing, changing or damaging effect. What is meant is the ability to carry out an action that affects the inner or essential core of a matter or structure. In the narrower sense, it is often understood as an (illegitimate) exercise of coercion. The will those over whom violence is exercised is disregarded or broken (English force, Latin vis or violen-tia). In a sociological sense, violence is a source of power (not fainting). "(German Wikipedia)

One can see violence as a wrong means of survival (except for self-defense).

"Violence" in the sense of violence can be found again in terms such as state authority or administration. The **separation of powers** is a fundamental organizational and functional principle of the <u>Constitution on Rule of law</u>. It means that one and the same institution is fundamentally <u>not allowed</u> to exercise different functions of authority, the different areas of jurisdictionstate violence assigned. But it also means that the same person may not belong to different institutions. Based on the historical model, a distinction is made between the three powers:

- **legislation (<u>legislative branch</u>)**
- **case law (<u>judiciary</u>)**
- **executive force (<u>executive</u>)**

The distribution of state power over several State organs serves the purpose of **power-limitation and securing of freedom and equality**. "(Quoted from Wikipedia)

Zivil law and criminal law are based on the general prohibition of violence. The only exceptions are situations of self-defense and emergency (against violence and torture, for arrest (including German §127 StPO), for rape (= penetration with force), for assistance, in domestic law) and cases of immediate compulsion of enforcement officers of the (legal) state. The use of violence in education is prohibited in Germany. "(Wikipedia)

If violence is to be used, it should be proportionate. (this is to practice by Personal)

P.S. A more vegetarian diet leads to a decrease in acts of violence in the affect ...

The following graphic is a diagram of how the process for getting rich is structured:

p. 39

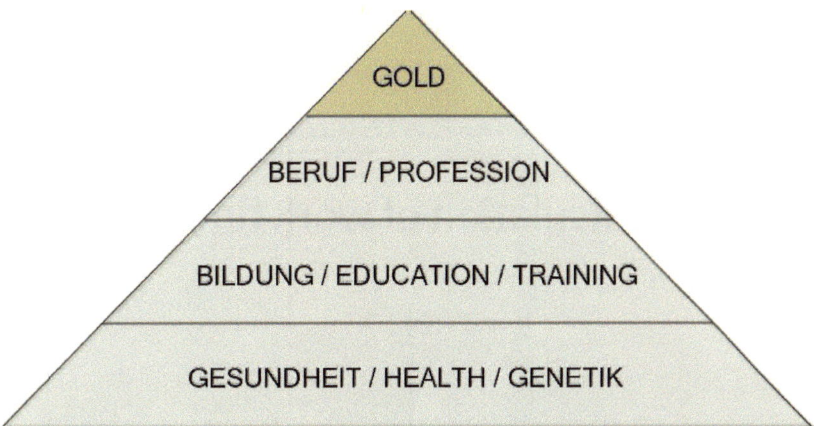

The process is the development to a valuable person ("human capital") from bottom to top "bottom up", whereby everything has to be healthy first (see chapter health), then school and education (see chapter school), then the exercising the learned profession at work (see chapter work), which then leads to wealth … which one can then use accordingly (see chapter money) …. so you shouldn't concentrate on gold beforehand …

Everyone is the maker of their happiness through their activity (in terms of quantity and quality)

<u>**Job:**</u>

"In physics, work is the energy that is mechanically transferred from one body to another, in that a force acts on it along a path. The unit of measurement is joules or newton meters "(Wikipedia). Accordingly, at first glance, only physical work would be real work, but energy also flows during intellectual work, but it is not obvious to everyone ...

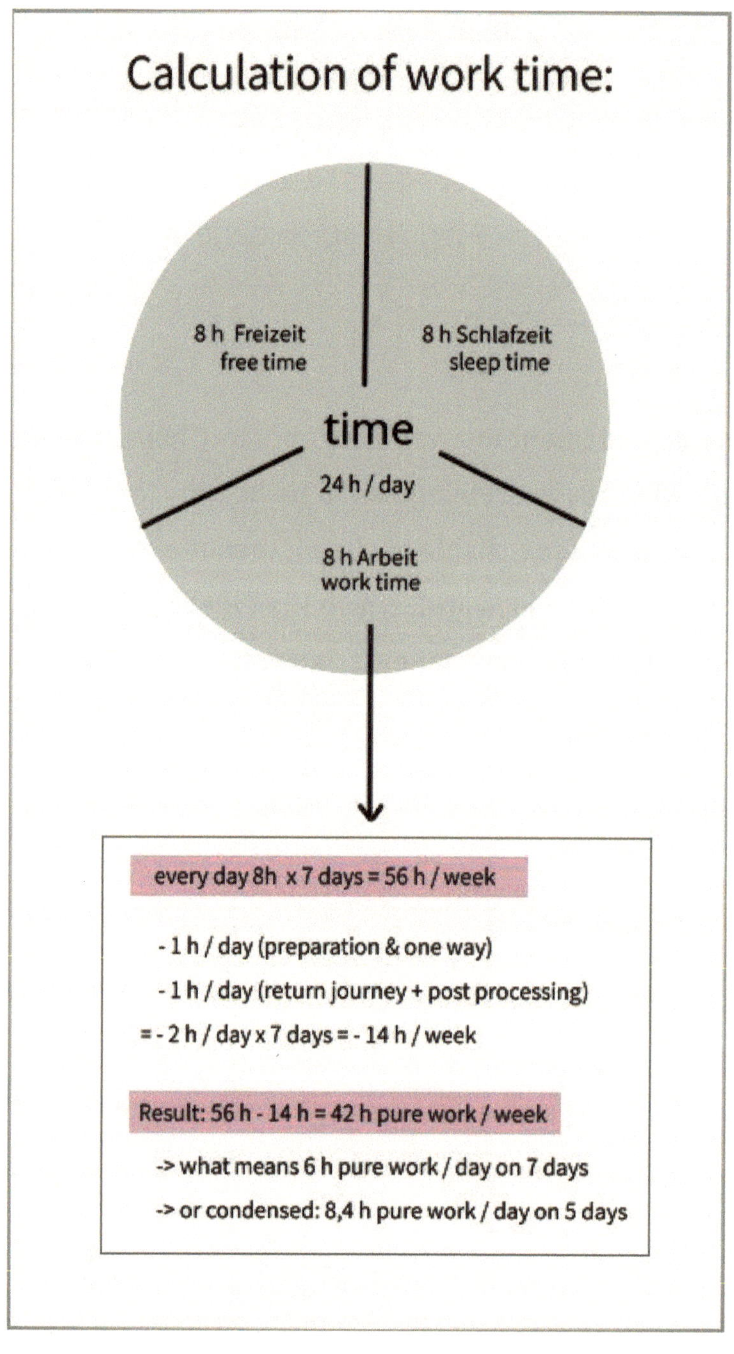

"Work is half life" is not true, because you live when you sleep ...

The person is crucial for the professional role in life. The job should match genetics ("test") so that one is able to practice it very well. One should have positive feelings at work as motivation. You can look for a role model whose work you like. According to "Maslow", self-realization is at the top of the hierarchy of needs; this is possible through suitable work.

In order to do a professional job, you first need training - this serves to be able to do something in which you can get a professional qualification. After the training it makes sense to work in practice. With the appropriate qualifications in one area, you can demand money from others for your work, which is a livelihood - this strengthens personality and self-esteem. It is important if the work is paid accordingly with money so that one can feed oneself, art without a job does not bring anything financially at all. Unpaid work is rewarded with sympathy by others, but you can also be disappointed. It is important that everyone gets exactly the money for their work that is worth it,

How could one evaluate work financially? According to qualification, status, experience, occupational groups, work performance, responsibility, years of service, economic achievement or in equal parts to all and who will judge that ...?

When you work, you should focus on the job, not the money. It is better to concentrate on one thing than on several at the same time. Goal-oriented work is important to get the job done in the shortest possible time. If you do the work carefully, you have a clear conscience.

Satisfaction from something achieved is good. 100% performance is only possible if you feel in top shape - that's why work is based on health, which always comes first. A "healthy" private life (see chapter health) promotes work immensely. It should be an obligation for companies to maintain the health of their workers in the long term with appropriate equipment (e.g. knee pads, back supports) so that the workers can perform at 100% over a long period (approx. 50 years). Healthy workers bring more in the long term than worn out and damaged workers - as an entrepreneur one can often ask oneself where "the shoe pinches" for a worker to eliminate the problem, which leads to a profit. In addition, this precaution also relieves the entire health and financial system, since there are fewer elderly sick people;

For work you often need appropriate clothing every day that shouldn't be dirty and worn. If the clothes get dirty every day at work, you need a separate wardrobe for each day, i.e. several identical "uniforms", which you then wash all together at the end of the week.

If the clothes are torn and have holes, you could mend them immediately on the same evening or replace them (let the boss) with ident parts.

The costs for the cloakroom and its cleaning (here in Germany a flat rate of 110 €) can either be stated independently as income-related expenses in the tax return or they are borne by the employer (who may be insured accordingly), as long as they are required by law for security.

"Job addiction describes the clinical picture of a person for his (supposed) well-being, his ostensible health and satisfaction or his apparent success from the exercise of work in the medical sense dependent people and ... is thus a "material-independent addiction", In which an obsessive attitude towards performance and work is developed, with all the medical and psychological consequences and secondary illnesses known from other addiction disorders. Work addicts live more or less exclusively for their work. The focus is mostly on quality and quantity, but not the meaning or purpose of the work to be done and it becomes one perfectionist basic attitude implemented. " (German Wikipedia)

Child labor is prohibited (see human rights), as children are growing and physical work can damage their health.

An unconditional basic income should only be available for people who are unable to work. It would be desirable to have an information system that shows where what work is needed - the inputs could be made by the citizens. In the end, work is always more constructive than waging war ...

Is the place of residence close to the workplace -> save (transfer) costs and time!

<u>**Craft:**</u>

"Craftsmen used to group themselves in so-called guilds, guilds or collieries, which represented a corporate body of craftsmen. "The Latin expression for these associations was college." The external identification was coats of arms, symbols and guild clothing. "The guilds controlled the number of craftsmen and journeymen in the cities and put their rules in writing in officially approved guild regulations firmly. In this way, the rules of the respective trades were drawn up and monitored, for example training rules, working hours, product quality and prices. In this way they ensured that there was not too much competition within a city. Internally, the guilds had the right of self-administration, so the masters regulated their financial affairs independently, chose their heads ("elders", old masters and young masters) themselves, in some cases also had the journeyman's coffers in custody, were able to impose fines and collect fines, so they owned certain things commercial police powers. In addition to their economic function, the guilds also performed religious, social, cultural and military tasks. In the event of serious illness or death, the master families received support from the official ark. "" Guilds owned on the work they didprivileged were, a monopoly". With the end of the guilds in the 19th century as a result of industrialization and the introduction of trade freedom, this was followed by de-privatization and the removal of vocational training from the guilds, since the organization of vocational training was now regulated by the state. Nowadays the successors of the guilds are craft guilds. "Membership in a German guild is voluntary; on the other hand, membership in the chamber of crafts for craftsman mandatory ". The handicrafts register is a directory in which the owners of companies that require authorization and the handicrafts they are to operate craft are to be entered. The handicraft role is held by the chambers of crafts guided. Theself-employed operation of a craft subject to authorization asstanding trade is only permitted to the natural and legal persons and companies entered in the craft register - these are mostly master craftsmen. "(German Wikipedia)

In order to master a craft masterfully, you need an apprenticeship (in which you learn the craft from a master), as well as a collection of experience in the journeyman's time, after which you can take the master's examination. With the completion of the master craftsman examination, you can become independent and open a business.

Typical craft trades: Carpenter, plumber, glazier, locksmith, painter, blacksmith, tailor, shoemaker, mechanic, baker, butcher, gardener, farmer, weaver, porter, sculptor, stonemason, fisherman, miller, silk maker, technician, optician, acoustician, chimney sweep, insulator , varnisher, confectioner, hairdresser, butcher

Tools and materials: In the trade you need the know-how which tool + material you use how, for what purpose. The tool itself has quality differences in terms of the resulting performance and usability. The handle and size of the tool is also very important because it is where the force is exerted on the tool. The handle is the focal point and should have a relatively soft texture (soft rubber, cork) in order to be able to exert as much pressure as possible from the hand on the tool. Good tools are more expensive than cheap ones. There are special tools for each area of application (such as wood, iron or concrete drills), which you should definitely pay attention to, because only with them the manual work can be carried out well and correctly, otherwise errors, accidents and possibly destruction of the tool. When using machines, the choice of machine for the specific area of application must be taken into account. There is a difference between using a drill or a hammer drill to drill a hole, depending on the material to be machined. Other factors play a role in machines: performance, size, usability, applicability, flexibility, setting options, energy supply (electricity, battery, fuel), description, availability, storage, maintenance, spare parts, service and purchase price. When buying tools, you can pay attention to quality seals or standardized norms. If you only need special tools for a short time, you can borrow them. If you need the tool again and again, you should buy it. For standard tools (screwdriver, hammer, pliers), which one you have for your entire life, you can buy a very good one straight away. Also with the consumables (screws, nails) you should pay attention to the purpose for which it is used (for example: wooden nails or steel nails) ...

<u>Pun measure</u>:

The smaller something is, the less it has in general in weight and the more important (in German language „wichtig") it is … (compare the German word „Wicht"), but less significant it´s measure . The bigger something is, the more it has in general in weight, the less important it is (compare the German word „Wicht") – but often the more important its measure. The measure is used to assess the importance of a thing: Great things are great. Small things have small dimensions. However, one often begins with important little things, which then grow through education and care and become larger and more signifiacnt over time … because something big and significant arises from something small and important, the "small" is sometimes particularly important…

<u>Ethics and craftsmanship are interesting</u>:

(One could do a study of craftsmen using the IQ.)

The craftsman should actually just do his job (for at least 20 $ / per hour after taxes)

<u>Pension for craftsmen</u>: As self-employed craftsmen often do not have a pension in the form of a pension, which is why many craftsmen try to buy real estate and build a house themselves cheaply in 45rdert o later rent one part and live on the other part from the rental income …

Idea: A common switching center for making appointments for local craftsmen …

<u>**Architecture:**</u>

The architecture of houses differs from country to country. German houses look different than Italian or Spanish houses, for example. The typical American houses are mostly made of wood. Japanese or Chinese houses are different. Feng-Shui is used there.

It is nice when the customary culture can be seen in the building of houses and you can also recognize a little the **individuality** of the residents. It is unpleasant when all houses look the same due to rationalization. Since man is an individual, he would also like to have his own individual house and not the same living room as everyone else, as is the case with an insect colony. This has often been done in the big cities in particular (apartment blocks). Small communities pay more attention to their cityscape ... many small houses around the globe are as a whole safer from force majeure than a few large houses, but sometimes you want to centralize something. When centralized by a building that is supposed to represent a hierarchy, I see a straight circular cone as one of the best buildings. Skyscraper, like the Tower of Babel have already fallen over. Very flat buildings are the safest, but they cost a lot of land and do not represent anything: they are not clearly seen from a distance ...

A **database** of local houses would be good for planning: With year of construction, construction plan, building material, building site, building style, construction costs, renovations, useful life. If you have statistics about how long houses stand in a certain area before they are demolished again, you would know beforehand how long the house will be in operation and what material you will then use in building ...

Local environmental conditions should be taken into account when constructing the buildings. **Environmentally friendly materials** and technology should be used in all modern homes. The most important thing when building a house is the location of the property, the size and architecture of the house and the associated costs ...

A market with cheap, recycled material from old buildings would also be interesting.

<u>**Money:**</u>

Money is "the means to an end" to finance existence and certain joys of life, but not the center of life, since the human being (the living being) is in the center and not money. One should not confuse the joy of living through buying something beautiful with money, with the joy of being healthy and alive, which is the basis for everything, but for which you also need money ... money can make you happy because it improves the external living conditions a lot – to get it for his (work) performance (in Germany ~ 3,000 € before taxes / per month for men) is satisfactory and you can avert many a misfortune – in the poor house you will certainly not be happy. Money should be handled well – neither wasteful for unnecessary things (luxury), nor too stingy for necessary things (not the cheapest) – and invest it well: Maybe first in your own apartment (so you don't have to pay rent) and then in stocks that have risen over the long term (approx. 12 years) or in a life insurance (so that someone (dear) is covered in the event of death). Financial discipline is to divide the money that will last until the end of life. Spending money (pocket money) on fun is fun (for the kids). Tip: Always have a cash reserve ($ 5,000 – $ 25,000) for repairs, maintenance, specialists, lawyers and doctors. To have a good feeling you should try to pay for all things yourself, debts and financial dependency create bad feelings (unhappy). "Money is time" means it is a matter of experience; therefore a school subject "money" would be very useful for young people, in which they learn how to deal with money.

Often you get money through partners, especially in the private sector through marriages (and marriage contracts) and inheritance (here this includes the will and the inheritance contract, otherwise the legal succession and ultimately always the compulsory portions).

It is not at all wrong if, from a financial point of view, you also think of your descendants (heirs) and not claim everything for yourself and spend it beforehand.

P.S. Inflation (devaluation due to rising prices) could be avoided by people still having more money through savings (meat, transfer, energy)

Note: Agent "Mark Hood" "Treasury" made "Intertrust".

Appreciation
according to German inheritance and tax law

for spouce, partner	100 %
for every child	80 %
for every grandchild	40 %
for every parent	20 %
for every brother or sister (why not 50 % ?)	4 %
for every one else	4 %

The graphic below is an example of how money can be used:

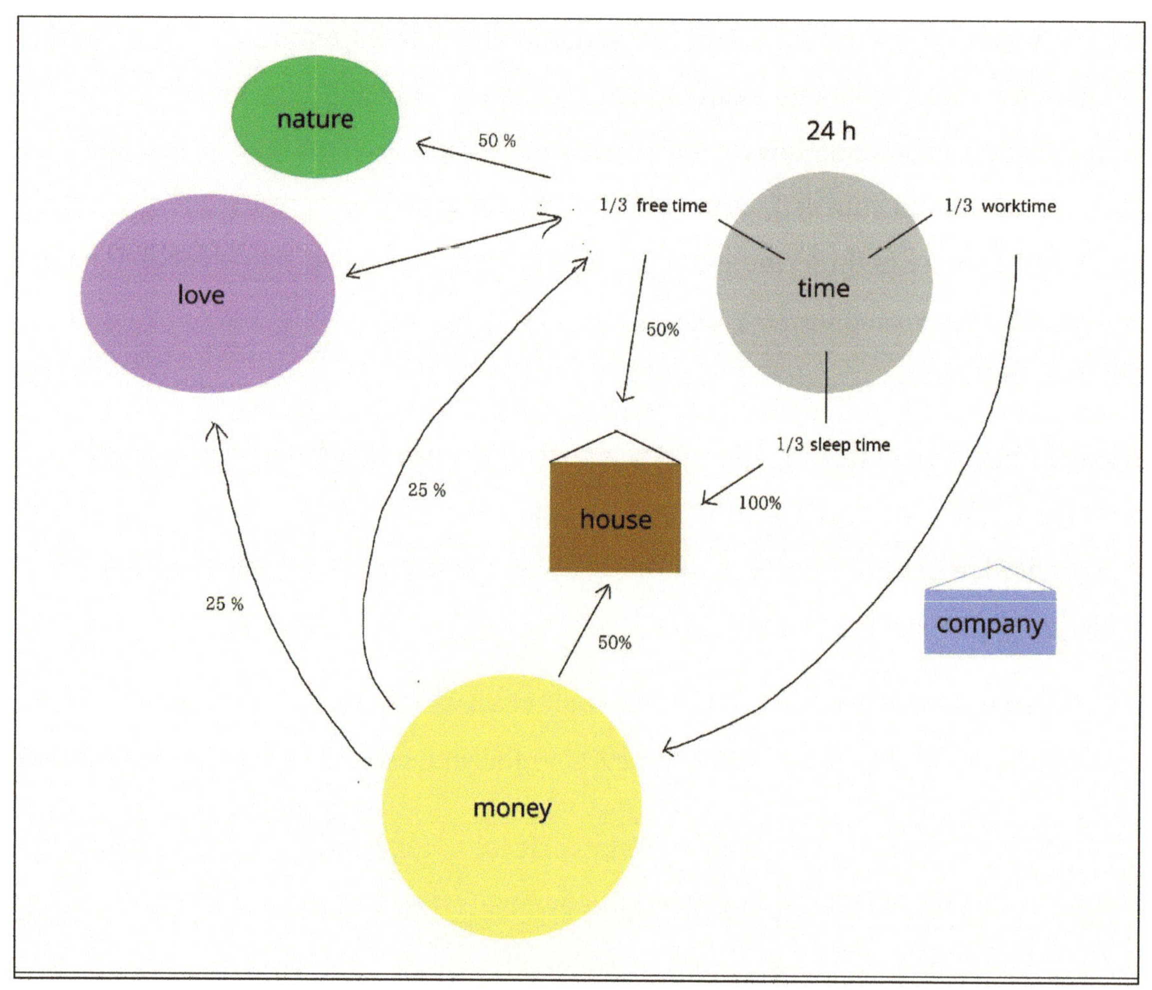

PS: If payment transactions are interrupted because of the weekend, this means a 2/7 loss of liquidity (28.57%)!

Taxes:

In order to **finance the state with its infrastructure** (land, roads, buildings), offices and servants (civil servants) (debts, fixed costs, investments, pensions), taxes (money from the population) must be levied on something ...

This can be used to <u>regulate the financial resources</u> (and the lives) of sections of the population.

If someone lives and / or works in a country, he / she also has to pay taxes, whereby correct accounting and information must be complied with promptly. Tax figures should be processed with the help of computer technology.

If the taxes seem too high, you can vote for another government in the next election or leave the country and live / work somewhere else (which has been possible in the EU for some time – see „Schengen Agreement" ...)

The control system should initially be simple (with good input), but then very detailed in order to be as individual (and therefore precise) as possible ...

The tax terms (definition) should also be understandable for normal people.

Taxes should be transparent to the citizen. It doesn't hurt to know everything about taxes: How high are your own taxes and what happens to them? Good explanations of tax collection are welcome – taxes could be named in such a way that it is immediately obvious in which area they flow – for example: environmental tax benefits the environment. This creates transparency for citizens regarding the payment and use of taxes and thus less criticism of the government. Taxes should only be used by the government to the best of its knowledge and belief. Tax embezzlement and waste should be criminalized.

One can also ask whether taxes shouldn't be the only source of money for the state, since the government, as legislator, should play a neutral role in the economy and not "make the law for itself"....

(Note: If only one religion receives taxes, it is not in the constitution.)

List of German taxes (in 2015):

Tax name:	Percentage:	Note:
Sales tax (VAT)	19% on the price of the goods	or 7% = reduced (books)
Input tax	19% on the purchase price	or 7% = reduced (books)
Corporate tax	15% on the profit	+ Solidarity surcharge 5.5%
Income tax	14% - 45% on income	Allowance: ~ 9,000 €
Income tax (source code)	by tax class	= Advance payment on the income tax
Capital gains tax (source tax)	25% + other	= Advance payment on the income tax
Supervisory board tax (source tax)	30% of the remuneration	= Advance payment on the income tax
Inheritance tax	7-50% according to tax class	Allowances / Exceptions
Gift tax	7-50% according to tax class	Allowances / Exceptions
Property tax	1% of the property	abolished
Property tax	according to the standard value + rate of assessment	
Church tax	8-9 % of income tax	
Business tax	according to trade income	Allowance: € 24,500 for pers.
Real estate transfer tax	3.5 - 6.5% (by country)	from the purchase price + other
Insurance tax	19%	Exceptions (LV, RV, KV)
Energy tax (mineral oil tax)	65.45 cents / liter of gasoline	47.04 cents / liter of diesel
Vehicle tax	according to cubic capacity + emissions	Vehicle owner tax
Electricity tax (eco tax)	2.05 cents / KWh	reduced at prod. Commercial
Tobacco tax	75% of the purchase price	per cigarette (box)
Liquor tax	according to alcohol volume	for spirits + 15% Alc.
Coffee tax	€ 2.19 / kilogram	also for EU purchases
Sparkling wine tax	€ 1.02 / 0.75 liters	Sparkling wine / sparkling wine
Beer tax	9.4 cents / liter	according to liters and original wort
Beverage tax (Liquor tax)	5%	abolished
Lottery tax / sports betting	20% / 5%	also horse racing
Fire protection tax	~ 2.85%	of (household) insurance
Dog tax	0 - 186 € / year per dog	by municipality (municipality)
Amusement tax	according to price + number	Event, sex, play car.

<u>**Possession:**</u>

A goal in life is to have financial independence from other people and **own property** without debt. That creates a **positive feeling**.

Debt burdens property if one is liable with it …

Land ownership is particularly important, as people who do not own land live in the property of other people, which creates negative feelings among tenants.

Owning a small house for every family ("social housing") should be a goal in the government's political program. Then there are fewer difficulties….

Wisdom: "Small but mine" (no landlords, creditors, lenders, lenders)

It is just as important to own things yourself or to be the owner instead of leasing them.

It is good to keep your property in good shape: Maintain, clean, clean, renovate, because the property won't break and you can benefit from it for longer.
Appreciation and value retention are good. In Japan, for example, you have to put on slippers before entering the house so that you don't dirty the house with your street shoes….

> However, it is also not right to distinguish yourself only through material possessions, since the focus is on people …

Products:

A "product" here means an economic product (goods, service) and not a product from mathematics (the result of certain links) or from chemistry (substance resulting from a chemical reaction). "In the business administration a material good or an (intangible) service understood that the result of a production processis - however, these are to be separated, even if they are often summarized in statistics as with gross domestic product ... the word is often used for a physical product product used synonymously. "(Wikipedia)

To improve products: "The devil is in the details" (music, pharmaceuticals, electronics)

There are mass products (in large numbers), series products (in variants), niche products (small market share) and individual products (individually manufactured).

The product components lie in a core property and function, additional properties, packaging, as well as basic and additional services.

The product types can be divided into physical goods of consumption (consumption and use) and industry (various), as well as services (consumptive and investment). The (multilingual) product description can be technical (drawing, CAD data), commercial (with a unique ID number - with the help of certain numbering), use-related (instructions for the buyer), maintenance and repair-related (for workshops) or marketing-oriented (to address potential customers).

Complementary products ("complement each other"), product design (design of series products), production resources (required work and operating resources), product development (developing and constructing a marketable product, with systematics and methods complementing the intuitive procedure) are still being discussed, Product life cycle (market launch (mostly) of a consumer good until it is removed), substitute products (interchangeable replacement) and universal design (can be used by many people without special adaptation). (Wikipedia)

You should first know what you want (needs), then look at product tests, read reviews, choose the product and buy it cheaply.

<u>**Economy:**</u>

According to Wikipedia: "Economy or economy is the totality of all facilities and actions that the planned satisfaction of needs serve…

"The need for economic activity arises from the scarcity the goods… "

Idea: Central EU warehouse (center in DEU) with cheap (EU) goods for supply.

In popular parlance, an economy is also called a pub or restaurant, since nutrition is the most important thing for many people (as with animals). Since people then also eat animal meat (which affects them), a kind of spiral has developed that gets bigger and bigger the more people there are, which overloads the planet …

The model should not be a Tyrannosaurus Rex that eats up everyone else …

But: "The meaning of life is to live" – an economy is necessary for this …

A distinction is also made between economics and business administration.

Economics describes the totality of all economic subjects in a space. The performance (GDP, national income), distribution, price development, structure, unemployment, and foreign trade are considered. To do this, one looks at the economy and its cycles and makes a comparison with others (including an overall economic account).

Free market economy: An exchange of goods between countries can be very useful if the countries have specialized in something in order to gain a common advantage, cf. Adam Smith book: "the wealth of nations" …

Social market economy: The social component in the market economy should help workers and employees to have health, pension, unemployment and long-term care insurance, so that they are covered and there are no grievances, as in the industrial revolution of the past. What is important is a broad middle class in society that forms a buffer between rich and poor.

Planned market: Didn't work because no progress was made….

 deals with the economy in companies. "The objectives are the description, analysis, explanation and support ... of decision-making processes in companies."

The goal of every company is to generate profit (for its own existence through money). The following aspects must be taken into account:

Starting a new company makes sense if you have developed a new product, for example software, otherwise not, as there are already many long-established competitors. Setting up a business in the local area makes sense if there are enough free customers and little competition on site. The **price-performance ratio** of the product / service plays a major role in the success on the market, but there you should behave "normally" with regard to prices in order to avoid irritation from the competition.

In a global economy with the same purchase prices of raw materials for all companies, personnel costs are decisive for total costs and profit. <u>The location with the suitably qualified staff</u> (and their cost of living) must be taken into account when planning the company. The company structure should be solid due to the stability. The pyramid is better suited than the tower and yet contains a certain hierarchy – the <u>circular cone</u> is even better. When building, you should start from the bottom, so spend money there first. Advertising: Prices for TV advertising are determined by a panel measurement and a corresponding extrapolation of the audience figures; it would be better to actually measure the <u>number of hits (on the Internet)</u>. For craft businesses (master craftsmen), word of mouth is often what counts ...

<u>Others</u>: With regard to the stock exchange, the number of shares in companies should be standardized so that share prices can be better "compared".

<u>Tip:</u> According to the nutritional recommendations in this book with salads, noodles + digestif, the housewives could register a noodle trade as a small side business (observe regulations) to buy the (best) noodles cheaply / cheaply from (Italian) specialist retailers (metro, wholesale market, industrial park) – (possibly also through import) and to be able to resell ...

<u>**Pension:**</u>

One of the advantages of retirement is that many people have a pension because people from the lower classes do not want to take care of their old age.

What speaks against the pension is that the costs are getting higher and higher due to demography. There are also administrative costs. Citizens could be obliged to take out (additional) private insurance, but if the insurance company goes bankrupt, the trouble and the costs are great....

As additional income for retirees, one could create **age-appropriate jobs** (such as counseling and apprenticeship training) that take into account the physical and mental circumstances of the elderly. Their experience in unchangeable things should play a role ...

It would be a good **idea** to **settle retirees** in a large "pack" (1,000 people) in a place **in another** European **country** (for example Hungary) where the cost of living is much lower than in Germany. The pensioners would then get a lot more for their money (bigger house / apartment, garden) and could lead **a better life** (e.g. go to dinner much more often per week), even if the other living conditions (e.g. medical care & care) were still normal have standard, but no longer high-tech like in Germany. By moving large groups together, everyone has company. In addition, "older ideas" and thinking would have been relocated and younger ones would have more opportunities in Germany, also with regard to living space.

<u>Old town idea:</u>

If that is undesirable, one could also create a whole city (district) with the same criteria for old people in Germany, where German is the mother tongue, especially in (technical) terms of old age, as well as walking, visual and hearing impairments: barrier-free, stair-free, flat short distances to shops, easier operation. Advantage: You don't have to (expensive) rebuild everything ...

Publisher: BoD · Books on Demand GmbH, In de Tarpen 42,
22848 Norderstedt
Print: Libri Plureos GmbH, Friedensallee 273,
22763 Hamburg
ISBN: 978-3-7583-6599-7